VANCOUVER
AND THE LOWER MAINLAND FROM THE AIR

VANCOUVER
AND THE LOWER MAINLAND FROM THE AIR

Photographed by Russ Heinl
Text by Constance Brissenden

Whitecap Books
Vancouver / Toronto / New York

Whitecap Books
Vancouver/Toronto/New York

Edited by Elaine Jones
Proofread by Elizabeth McLean
Cover design by Susan Greenshields
Interior design by Margaret Lee

Archival images courtesy of the B.C. Archives and Records Services: p. 13 I-21722; p. 22 I-21730; p. 32 I-27896; p. 45 HP-039068; p. 50 HP-095735; p. 54 H-06774 photo by De Mara; p. 59 I-28133; p. 63 I-27950; p. 64 HP-041265; p. 68 D-07253; p. 72 I-27897; p. 76 HP-060807; p. 90 G-00320; p. 100 I-28090; p. 104 B-00278; p. 106 E-06858; p. 111 G-04642

Printed in Canada.

Canadian Cataloguing in Publication Data

Brissenden, Constance, 1947–
    Vancouver and the Lower Mainland from the Air

    Includes index.
    ISBN 1-55110-958-1

    1. Vancouver (B.C.)—Aerial photographs. 2. Lower Mainland (B.C.)—Aerial photographs. I. Heinl, Russ, 1949– II. Title.
FC3847.37.B735 1999   917.11'33'00222   C99-910836-0
F1089.5.V22B75 1999

The publisher acknowledges the support of the Canada Council for the Arts and the Cultural Services Branch of the Government of British Columbia for our publishing program. We acknowledge the financial support of the Government of Canada through the Book Industry Development Program for our publishing activities.

Dedication

by Russ Heinl

For outstanding relatives who have unconditionally supported and loved my family throughout our lives. It is time each of you had some long over-due recognition for your unselfish and unquestioning support of all that we do. On behalf of me and my wife Anne, our son Matthew and our daughter Megan, from the bottom of our hearts, thank you all so very, very much to:

Kathy and George Calder

Molly and George Duncanson

Annie and Johnnie Rennie

Rita and Billy Wood

Introduction

by Constance Brissenden

Eagles soar over Vancouver, their eyes keen enough to pick out a dime on the ground two football fields away. Alas, the human eye is not so sharp. When we fly, the earth below, its habitats and inhabitants, speeds past. We see momentarily, then the image is gone.

That is why we can thank aerial photographer Russ Heinl for this book. Relying on a discerning eye and decades of photographic experience, Heinl provides surprising and fresh views of Vancouver and the surrounding region. Using gyro-stabilized cameras that compensate for the vibrations of the helicopter, he captures the scenes below, both natural and artificial.

Seen through Heinl's lens, the one overriding characteristic of Vancouver — its natural setting — takes on an entirely new perspective. His images range far afield, encompassing nearby mountains, seascapes and even the confluence of the Fraser and Thompson rivers in the Fraser Canyon, 175 kilometres away.

But Heinl gives us more than glimpses of these spectacular settings. His work allows us to study in detail sites that remain inaccessible to earthbound travellers. En route to Whistler along Highway 99, if you look sharp, you can catch a glimpse or two of Black Tusk in Garibaldi Provincial Park. In Heinl's aerial photograph, the icy splendour of the peak is so close you almost feel a chill.

Nature's presence determines a west coast lifestyle and mentality. We toil, but with the knowledge that the outdoor playground is only minutes away from office high-rises. Never was this fact more obvious than in the images shown here. We see the Pacific Ocean lapping against Vancouver's many beaches; the Fraser River winding through a dozen communities. Towering above all are the Coast Mountains.

Heinl also captures a more elusive phenomenon: the different quality of light, seen from the air. The afternoon sun softly brushes the tips of West Vancouver high-rises. The Lions Gate Bridge is bathed by the setting sun in golden tones. Over English Bay, a flaming sunset torches the Pacific Ocean. Below, the bow light of a freighter is a lone beacon against the darkening seas.

We see the urban landscape from a new perspective too. Glass-clad office towers give way to neatly ordered, tree-lined neighbourhoods. On the docks, heaps of yellow sulphur and orange cranes vibrate with the colours of an artist's palette. Freighters take on cargo, then dwarf the tiny tugs that shepherd them out to sea. From the air, the railway yards form a surprising contrast to the elegant swag of the Lions Gate Bridge nearby. Beyond city and industry lie the neatly arranged fields of the soil-rich delta lands.

Other photographs leave us marvelling at the inventiveness of humanity. By day, Vancouver is excitement, order, growth. By night, the city lights up like a sparkler. Looking down, familiar landmarks take on new dimensions. The curve of the Vancouver Public Library's coliseum-like walls and the peaks of the chateau-style roof of the Hotel Vancouver rise out of shadows. The white columns of the Vancouver Art Gallery, the cone-shaped roof of the Vancouver Museum and the glittering dome of Science World catch the light. In Stanley Park, eight carved totem poles cast long shadows. In the east end of the city, a ferris wheel at the Pacific National Exhibition whirls round and round. A fiery aerial act at the Abbotsford International Airshow is even more dramatic when seen from above.

From the historical perspective, the juxtaposition of archival photos and modern aerials is fascinating. Heinl has included seventeen black-and-white archival photographs of the region. Returning to their exact locations, he has painstakingly rephotographed these scenes. Some are vastly changed; others are remarkably similar.

In 1928, the Sea Island home of the future Vancouver International Airport was a patchwork of farmers' fields. Today, the airport handles more than 15 million passengers a year. In a 1930s photograph, a cruise ship navigates the First Narrows. Beyond, the villages of West Vancouver hug the shoreline. In the modern aerial, residential development marches inexorably up the flanks of the North Shore mountains. A 1940s photograph looking east from English Bay shows the West End as a tree-lined neighbourhood of wooden homes and low-rise apartment buildings. Today, amid the sea of high-rise apartments, a few original wood-frame buildings remain, classic reminders of a more genteel age. Archival photographs of the 1950s show a city experiencing a quantum change in the density and architecture of downtown. The few older buildings that remain evident in Heinl's recent pho-

tographs are links to the past in a fast-changing cityscape.

Some sites are surprisingly similar then and now. Coquitlam's Colony Farm, established in 1904 to treat the mentally ill with fresh air and hard work, exists today as Colony Farm Regional Park, a popular bird-watching site. The dramatic architecture of Vancouver City Hall, photographed from the air in 1954, is the same, although residential development has filled in around it and the surrounding trees have grown to impressive heights. Burnaby Mountain, prior to the opening of Simon Fraser University in 1965, was an unbroken forest. Today, a full-fledged university perches atop the mountain, but the surrounding forest is equally as lush.

Russ Heinl's distinctive aerials of the region prove to be the perfect foil for the evocative historical images. Past and present join forces to create a sweeping photographic overview of one of the world's most beautiful cities. The result is a new way of seeing that changes our perceptions of these familiar landscapes forever.

False Creek in the foreground winds its way into downtown Vancouver under the Burrard, Granville and Cambie street bridges. Once an eyesore of industrial decay and toxic waste, False Creek was given new life as the site of Expo 86. Today the area is a blend of residential housing, marinas, parks and restaurants. The white, Teflon-coated fibreglass roof of BC Place Stadium, one of the world's largest air-supported domes, is always easy to identify.

The panoramic 1958 view of the North Shore (above) reveals why outdoor aficionados have considered it a recreational mecca from the early part of the century onward. Grouse Mountain (where North America's first double chair-lift was built in 1949), then Hollyburn to the west and finally Seymour to the east, lured skiers looking for new slopes to conquer. The Lions Gate Bridge and Stanley Park remain a constant in both the archival and modern aerials.

Leaving Port Vancouver, an outbound luxury cruise ship passes under the Lions Gate Bridge past Prospect Point in Stanley Park. More than 220 cruise ship stopovers are recorded every year in Vancouver. The city is home port to the famed Vancouver-Alaska cruise; close to a million passengers a year enjoy this unique run, one of the most popular cruise destinations in the world.

En route to Alaska, passengers onboard the multi-tiered *Legend of the Sea* bask in the summer sun. From May to October, some of the world's largest ships make Vancouver a regular port of call as the southern terminus of the Vancouver-Alaska cruise. Ships are welcomed at Canada Place, built for Expo 86, and nearby Ballantyne Pier.

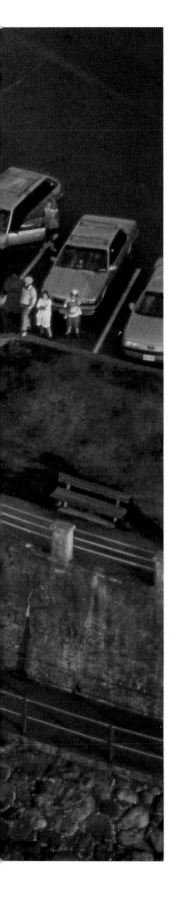

LEFT Strollers and cyclists on the Stanley Park Seawall pass by historic Brockton Point Lighthouse, named after HMS *Plumper* senior engineer, Francis Brockton, who surveyed the shoreline in the 1850s. The seawall was the dream of park commissioner M.S. Logan, who envisioned a walkway devoid of automobiles, offering views of harbour, mountains and forest. From 1917 until his death in 1963, Scottish stonemason James Cunningham devoted his life to its construction. On July 22, 1971, the last granite blocks of the ten-kilometre seawall were finally put in place.

ABOVE The Teahouse Restaurant overlooks historic Ferguson Point in Stanley Park. During World War II the area was the site of defense fortifications and the building was an officers' mess. When the Teahouse opened in the 1950s its managers lived in the building during the winter and served food through the summer months. Today it is an upscale restaurant that operates year-round.

At the formal dedication of Stanley Park in 1889, Canada's governor general, Lord Stanley, proclaimed that the park was "for the use and enjoyment of peoples of all colours, creeds and customs, for all time." Situated on a 405-hectare peninsula between English Bay and Burrard Inlet, it remains one of North America's largest and most impressive city parks. The eight totem poles at Brockton Point were carved by First Nations artists. The first pole was raised in 1924.

Then and Now

In 1958 Coal Harbour already reflected the outdoors lifestyle of west coast residents. Light industry along the foreshore took the form of marine works and boat sheds. Stanley Park provided moorage for the Burrard Yacht Club and was home to the Vancouver Rowing Club. Coal Harbour today is a busy waterway for pleasure craft, float planes and rowing skiffs. Deadman's Island (mid right), a First Nations' burial ground for victims of smallpox from 1888 to 1892, is now home to the naval station HMCS *Discovery*. The tower and pool of The Westin Bayshore (mid foreground) are surrounded by a massive redevelopment project on the former Canadian Pacific Railway yards.

Located in Stanley Park, the Vancouver Aquarium Marine Science Centre is home to more than 8000 species of aquatic life. Opened in 1956, the facility was Canada's first public aquarium and is now one of the largest in North America. In the water habitats seen here, a family of beluga whales swims together, while an orca shares a pool with a Pacific white-sided dolphin.

Summer weather beckons sun seekers to a string of sandy beaches along English Bay. Neatly aligned driftwood logs at Third Beach make perfect backrests.

LEFT Built as the Canada Pavilion for Expo 86, Canada Place features five Teflon-coated "sails." The nautical theme is ideal for the cruise ship terminus and Vancouver's trade and convention centre. The Canada Place promenade provides excellent views of Port Vancouver and cruise ships, seaplanes, the SeaBus, private yachts and other craft. The domed Pan Pacific Hotel in the foreground is one of several major hotels in the area.

ABOVE Bathed in the warm ochre tones of sunset, Vancouver's central library at 350 West Georgia Street is reminiscent of a Roman coliseum. The nine-storey structure, designed by Moshe Safdie and Downs/ Archambault, was completed in 1995. More than 8000 people pass through the library every day.

The Vancouver Art Gallery is housed in a former courthouse built in 1911 on Robson Square between Granville and Burrard. The gallery's impressive facade, emphasized by marble columns, adds historic interest to the city core. The wide steps are a popular place to sit and relax. Architect Francis Rattenbury also designed Victoria's Legislative Buildings and the Empress Hotel, as well as many Vancouver mansions.

Then and Now

In 1952 the downtown Vancouver skyline was dominated by two impressive structures. Centre stage in this photo is the massive Hotel Vancouver, with its distinctive steep roof. Visible behind the hotel, at 355 Burrard Street, is the 25-storey Marine Building, considered an architectural masterpiece when opened in 1930. Both buildings remain icons of Vancouver's cityscape, though now dwarfed by the skyscrapers around them. Burrard Street cuts a central swath through the downtown business centre, leading to Burrard Inlet and the white "sails" of Canada Place.

34

RIGHT Wall-to-wall glass curtain windows are a popular architectural feature of many downtown Vancouver high-rise office towers. The 21-storey Commerce Place, located on the east side of Burrard Street between West Pender and West Hastings streets, is one example, its tiered effect emphasized by the interplay of sun and shadow.

LEFT The Dominion Trust Building at Hastings and Cambie once boasted the title of tallest building in the British Empire. Built in 1908, the thirteen-storey edifice was renovated and now provides office space with old-world charm and low rents.

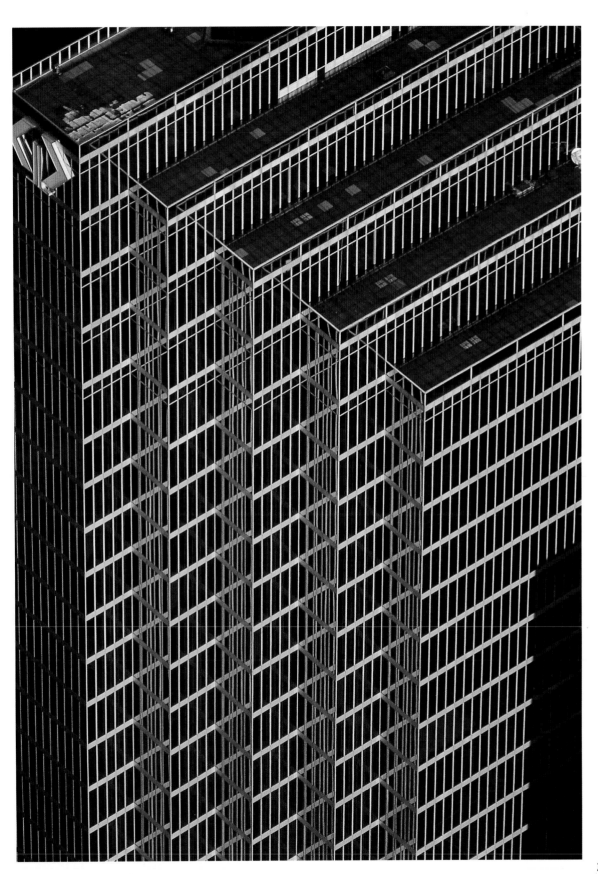

Nighttime Vancouver sparkles with lights from high-rise office towers. Trendy Robson Street, a diagonal line of lights from left to right, bisects the high-density West End residential area.

RIGHT The steep, chateau-style roof of the Hotel Vancouver at 900 West Georgia Street has been a city landmark since the 1930s. Due to the Depression, it took ten years to finish, opening in time for the 1939 visit of King George VI. Recently refurbished and renovated, it is run by Canadian Pacific Hotels.

LEFT Amid the office towers of downtown, the four-faced clock atop the seventeen-storey Vancouver Block (foreground) is a standout. Each face is nine metres in diameter. The three-metre-long minute hands move fifteen centimetres per minute. Built in 1912, the clock is a credit to traditional craftsmanship and still contains most of its original parts.

The elongated shadows of youthful soccer players loom in the late afternoon sun. Soccer is one of B.C.'s fastest growing sports; around 100 000 soccer players are registered in the province.

ABOVE Built for Expo 86 as the Expo Centre, Science World is now a popular family attraction. Inside the multi-million-dollar geodesic dome is the Alcan OMNI-MAX Theatre, with ten tonnes of sound equipment and one of the world's largest domed screens. Hundreds of hands-on exhibits attract half a million visitors each year. Located at the east end of False Creek, Science World is the centre of a new high-rise neighbourhood, City Gate.

RIGHT In a mere century, the West End of Vancouver has undergone a metamorphosis. In 1901, construction began on the forested, sloping shores of English Bay. Soon mansions for the rich and two-storey frame houses for the rest sprang up. By the late 1950s and early 1960s, the area's sandy beaches and tree-lined streets attracted a modern-day building boom which has resulted in one of the highest concentrations of high-rises in any Canadian city.

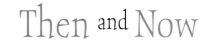

This archival photograph shows the West End in the 1940s, before the boom in high-rise development. The longer pier is in front of the boxy Sylvia Hotel; the small pier sits alongside Englesea Lodge, the only building on the beach side of Beach Avenue until it was destroyed by arson in 1981. The West End is now one of Canada's highest density neighbourhoods. A few of the original wood-frame homes are still tucked between the condominiums and apartments.

A freighter lies at anchor in English Bay, waiting to enter Port Vancouver. Frequently a dozen or more international freighters can be seen waiting in the bay.

St. Paul's Hospital on Burrard Street includes three main buildings, one of
which, the Burrard Building, is pictured here. In 1893, Mother Mary Theresa
of the Sisters of the Charity of Providence bought seven lots of land to build
the original St. Paul's, a 25-bed wood-frame hospital. The first patient was
admitted November 21, 1894. Today the facility accommodates more than 440
patients, is a major centre for AIDS, heart and renal care, and is rated one of
the 80 best hospitals in North America.

Then and Now

Shaughnessy Heights was named for CPR president (1898–1918) Thomas Shaughnessy. An upper-class enclave, Shaughnessy's palatial mansions were built on crescent streets that followed the contours of the terrain. By the 1920s, when this photo was taken, most of the city's society types had settled here. In the centre of the photo, just inside the outer crescent, is Hycroft, the 1909 mansion of industrialist Alexander Duncan McRae. The grounds included gardens, greenhouse, riding stables and tennis courts. Today a refurbished Hycroft opens to the public at Christmas. In both archival and present-day photographs, the Shaughnessy Crescent roundabout dominates the view. Today, Granville Street (foreground) leads to downtown Vancouver through the chic shopping area of South Granville.

Burrard Bridge (left) and Granville Bridge (right) cross False Creek to link South Granville with the city centre. Easily seen is the white roof of BC Place Stadium. The land along the north shore of False Creek, once the site of Expo 86, has been developed into a high-rise residential area.

Then and Now

In 1935, when Vancouver's new city hall opened, it was located far from the city centre on a slope at Cambie Street and 12th Avenue. Built during the Great Depression, the complex boasted Art Deco touches such as zigzag ornamentation below its windows. The August 1954 photo highlights the clean, cubic Moderne-style architecture. Today's city hall is largely unchanged. The front faces busy 12th Avenue; the rear (shown here) offers a small public park (bottom right). The tower's four-faced clock boasts red neon dials that are highly visible at night.

A marina nestles alongside the Granville Island dock while vehicles cross overhead on the Granville Bridge. Steps away from the dock, converted warehouses offer a variety of activities, including a huge public market, shops and live theatre. The yellow roof of Bridges Restaurant, one of many cafes and restaurants on the former industrial site, stands out.

Then and Now

In 1954 a new Granville Street bridge opened, high above industrialized Granville Island, False Creek and the obsolete swing-span bridge. In this 1950s archival aerial, log booms attest to the ongoing presence of lumber mills in the heart of the city. Twenty-five years later, a new Granville Island opened for business. Gone were the majority of industries. In their place, a mix of restaurants, shops, theatres and artists' studios has developed. In the modern photo, extensive marina facilities are evident between the Burrard Bridge (left) and the Granville Bridge. The island's centrepiece is the Granville Island market, to the right of the yellow roof.

ABOVE The Vancouver Museum and the Pacific Space Centre are located in Kitsilano's Vanier Park. The H.R. MacMillan Planetarium is located in the top of the central dome. The west wing (left) is home to the space centre; the remaining two wings showcase museum artifacts and displays. Visitors inevitably want to photograph *The Crab*, George Norris's stainless-steel sculpture, which presides outside.

RIGHT As newcomers from other parts of Canada as well as overseas settle in, the population of Vancouver increases every year. By the year 2001, the Greater Vancouver area will top two million residents, yet the city is characterized by its gardens and green spaces, enhanced by more than 100 000 trees planted by the Board of Parks and Recreation since 1916.

Established in 1915, the University of British Columbia was still mostly
potential when this photograph was taken in 1957. Many hectares of open
space remained undeveloped on its Point Grey campus. These spaces have
largely been filled with buildings that house more than 51 200 full- and
part-time students, making UBC the second-largest university in Canada.
Then, as now, log booms stretch along the north arm of the Fraser River.
The majority of the forested lands visible in this photograph is now
part of the 750-hectare Pacific Spirit Regional Park, established in 1988.

Then and Now

Burrard Inlet in 1946 was a busy port, one of the world's finest deep-water harbours. In the foreground is the original Second Narrows Bridge, which carried rail and automobile traffic before separate bridges for each were built. In the distance, Vancouver harbour curves toward Stanley Park. The twin landmarks of the Marine Building and Hotel Vancouver rise between Coal Harbour and English Bay. The modern aerial shows today's six-lane highway bridge, started in 1956 and completed four years later, with a cantilevered main span of 350 metres. During construction, the collapse of the north anchor arm killed eighteen men. In 1994, the bridge was renamed The Ironworkers Memorial Bridge in their honour but is commonly known as the Second Narrows Bridge.

RIGHT A bulk carrier is escorted out to sea by a tiny but powerful tractor tug. Along the British Columbia coast, a fleet of more than 200 tugs and 800 barges ensures that cargo reaches domestic markets and export terminals.

LEFT Orange gantry cranes are used to unload container vessels calling at Port Vancouver with cargo destined for Toronto, Montreal and elsewhere. Two of Port Vancouver's container facilities, Vanterm and Centerm, are situated on the inner harbour. Vanterm, a multi-purpose container terminal, also handles non-containerized cargoes such as newsprint, pulp and bulk oils. Centerm handles containers from some of the world's largest ships, moving pulp, lumber, steel products and specialized cargo.

Then and Now

Barnet Lumber Company, pictured here in the 1920s, was established in 1889 by Quebecker David McLaren, who dubbed it Barnet, his wife's maiden name. Though the sawmill was destroyed by fire in 1946, its castlelike scrap burner can still be seen on the shore of Barnet Marine Park, which occupies the site today. Located on Burrard Inlet, the park offers good swimming beaches, picnic sites, a launch for canoes and kayaks, and wooded areas.

North Vancouver's bulk handling terminals are part of a network that defines Vancouver as a major port. Here, piles of yellow sulphur stand out against the blue waters of Burrard Inlet. The port handles close to 10 000 vessel calls each year, of which 3000 are by foreign ships. Port Vancouver encompasses more than 150 kilometres of coastline and has twenty major terminals.

Then and Now

By 1952 when this archival photograph was taken, the Lions Gate Bridge was fourteen years old and already called obsolete. Built by the Guinness family for $5.7 million, the bridge — the longest suspension bridge in the British Empire at the time — made a 100 per cent profit. The family ran it as a toll bridge until they recouped their costs, then sold it to the provincial government for $6 million. Unlike residential West Vancouver, parts of North Vancouver have developed along industrial lines. The BC Rail yards (in the foreground of the modern photo) handle a wealth of the province's resources, including forest products, coal, minerals and metal concentrates. The railway offers passenger service as far as Prince George.

LEFT Pacific Coast Terminals Company Limited, located in Port Vancouver's inner harbour, handles about 3.5 million tonnes of yellow dry-bulk sulphur in a typical year. The glowing piles catch the eye at the dockside. About 35 per cent of the total world's trade in sulphur is exported through Vancouver.

RIGHT A BC Ferry on Howe Sound approaches the Horseshoe Bay terminal. Some 1000 people live in the hills around Horseshoe Bay, a twenty-minute drive from Vancouver. It was known to its Native inhabitants as Chai-hai, translated as a low sizzling noise, possibly from small fish jumping in the evening. Today the sounds are of cars rolling on and off the ferries on their way to Vancouver Island, the Sunshine Coast or Bowen Island. Nevertheless, Horseshoe Bay still retains a village ambiance.

Then and Now

A ship passes through the First Narrows in the 1930s, with the undeveloped North Shore in the background. For years, the quickest way to West Vancouver was by ferry boat, but this changed with construction of the Lions Gate Bridge over First Narrows in 1938. Ferry traffic was soon dramatically reduced, and by 1947 it stopped altogether. West Vancouver is an affluent municipality with nearly 2500 hectares of park and recreation land. The Park Royal Shopping Centre (far right) was the first shopping mall in Canada.

Thousands of bright lights twinkle on the Lions Gate
Bridge each night, adding to the beauty of the First
Narrows crossing. Completed in 1938, the bridge was
a noteworthy architectural achievement. Named for the
Lions, twin-peaked mountains that overlook Vancouver,
it is a cherished landmark. At its southern portal rest
two stone lions, carved by famed Italian immigrant
Charles Marega.

The enclosed gondola of the Grouse Mountain Skyride takes eight minutes to climb from 290 metres to 1211 metres above sea level. Grouse Mountain (named after the blue grouse) was one of the first ski areas developed near Vancouver. At the top is a display centre and restaurant complex.

The sun gleams on the towers of West Vancouver in this panoramic view looking across Burrard Inlet to Stanley Park and the city of Vancouver beyond.

Forty-four kilometres north of Horseshoe Bay at the head of Howe Sound, the town of Squamish is home to approximately 12 000 people. Its name means Mother of the Wind in the Coast Salish language. Not surprisingly, the area is known in North America as a premier wind-surfing destination, situated in a narrow corridor and surrounded by massive, sheer rock faces.

RIGHT The snow-covered peak of Black Tusk in Garibaldi Provincial Park towers over the route to Whistler. Summer hiking parties to Black Tusk have been popular since the early 1900s. Today, Garibaldi Provincial Park has a well-developed trail system and hardy summer hikers can make their way to alpine lakes and meadows.

LEFT Whistler Resort, located 120 kilometres north of Vancouver, is a perpetual winner in the annual ratings of prominent ski resorts. Its side-by-side mountains, Blackcomb (pictured here) and Whistler, both offer 1600 metres of vertical drop, but even the most non-athletic visitor will appreciate the excellent restaurants, lodgings and boutiques. Mountain biking and hiking in the summer make it a year-round resort.

Rising out of the snow, Chateau Whistler Resort sets the tone for Canada's premier ski destination. Whistler's architects look to European-style ski villages for their inspiration, incorporating cobbled walkways and plazas, boutiques, cafes and bistros into the design.

Then and Now

This 1928 photo was taken above the pastures of Sea Island, proposed home of Vancouver's new airport between the north and middle arms of the Fraser River. By 1932, a wood-frame terminal welcomed the first passenger flights from Seattle. Today, international flights landing at Vancouver International Airport fly over the heavily populated City of Richmond, seen in the modern photo, most of which exists south of Sea Island on larger Lulu Island. In 1998, Vancouver International Airport handled over 15 million passengers.

LEFT Two T-33 "T-bird" Silver Stars from Canadian Forces Base Comox 414 Combat Support Squadron practise formation flying over the Coast Mountains north of Howe Sound. The rugged Coast Mountain range, formed 80 million years ago, extends eastward to the interior plateaus and northward for 1700 kilometres to the Yukon.

ABOVE The photographer is almost eyeball-to-eyeball with the pilot of a two-seater, single-engine plane designed and built in Chilliwack, B.C. The model, Renegade Spirit, is one of five aircraft kits shipped throughout the world by Murphy Aircraft Manufacturing.

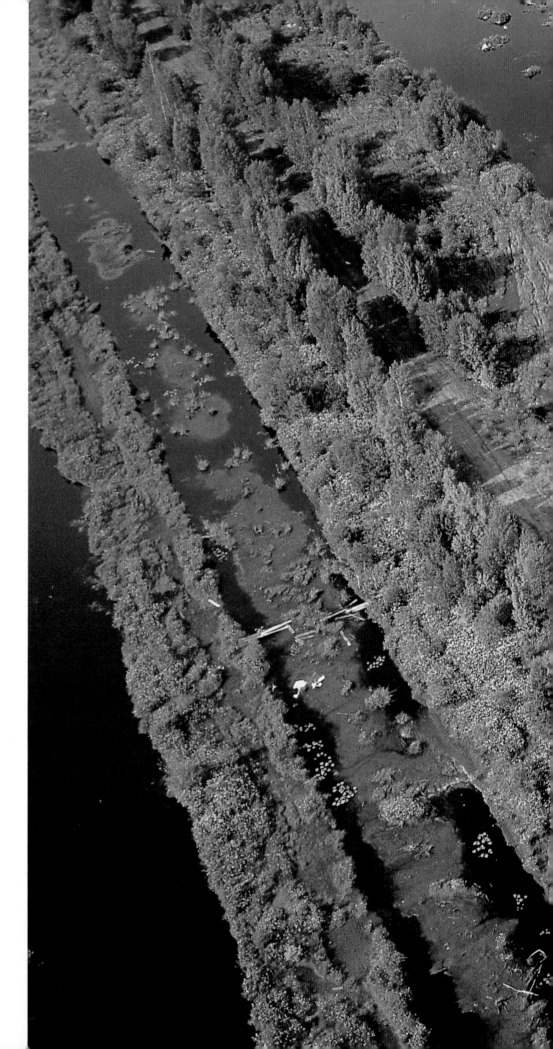

A decaying shack on Delta's Burns Bog is a remnant of
earlier times. At 4000 hectares, Burns Bog is the largest
greenbelt in the Lower Mainland and one of the largest
peat bogs in the world. Peatlands such as Burns Bog are
rare, found in only three per cent of the world. The bog's
wetlands support plants such as sphagnum moss and
Labrador tea and animals including deer, muskrat
and beaver.

With a population of more than 175 000, Burnaby is the third-largest city in the province. The towers of Metrotown, the largest of Burnaby's four town centres, dominate the low-rise apartments in the foreground. The elevated SkyTrain rapid transit guideway bisects the photograph.

The Pacific National Exhibition opens its gates from mid-August to Labour Day, featuring midway rides such as the 1924 ferris wheel.

Then and Now

In this archival photo, a clearing reveals the start of construction for the campus of Simon Fraser University, 365 metres above the Pacific Ocean on Burrard Mountain. The award-winning complex opened in 1965 and established the reputations of architects Arthur Erickson and Geoffrey Massey. Thirty minutes east of Vancouver, SFU remains North America's only mountaintop campus, overlooking city, suburbs and Burrard Inlet (top right in both photos). Beyond is a panoramic view of the Coast Mountains.

RIGHT Beyond the tip of Annacis Island, downtown New Westminster rises above the Fraser River. In its early days, Annacis Island was used for farming and fishing. It was later the site of an industrial park and today is home to a multi-million-dollar industrial estate occupying just over 445 hectares.

LEFT Burnaby Mountain is home to Simon Fraser University (right), where the Terry Fox sports field is an eye-catching green oval. in 1996, SFU, the City of Burnaby and Province of British Columbia completed the transfer of all land below the campus to the city to preserve as a park. The 576-hectare forest is now known as Burnaby Mountain Conservation Area. The view includes Vancouver and the North Shore.

Then and Now

When this photo was taken in 1950, the forested bank of the Fraser River in New Westminster was a tranquil setting for the Provincial Mental Hospital, a facility later known as Woodlands, and, to the right in the picture, a federal penitentiary. Woodlands is now closed; the penitentiary is the site of a housing project. The oldest of its buildings was retained and now houses doctors' offices. The original gatehouse is a coffee shop appropriately named The Gatehouse.

Then and Now

The archival photo shows residential New Westminster as it looked in the 1950s. Established as a port on the Fraser River, New Westminster was named by Queen Victoria and is still known as The Royal City. The arrival of SkyTrain light rapid transit in 1986 triggered a development boom: a waterfront promenade along the north side of the river curves past condominiums and the New Westminster Quay Market. In the lower half of both photographs is the eastern tip of Queensborough, which remains a pocket of farmland bordered by commerce and industry. To the left is little Poplar Island, undeveloped and heavily treed even today.

One-quarter of the world's cranberries are grown in rural areas around Vancouver. Cranberry bogs in Richmond, Pitt Meadows and Fort Langley produce 85 per cent of the average 17 million–kilogram crop each year. The main buyer is Ocean Spray Cranberries, a grower-owned cooperative.

In 1904, a large parcel of land in Coquitlam was set aside for a facility which included Essondale psychiatric hospital (the name later changed to Riverview) and Colony Farm, pictured here in the 1920s. The philosophy of the day was to treat mental illness with fresh air and hard work, both provided by labour in the gardens and barns of Colony Farm. For many years, the residents produced their own food, and their produce and livestock won prizes for their quality. Today the site of the old Colony Farm remains essentially rural. In 1995, it was agreed to set aside 113 hectares as a wildlife preserve called Colony Farm Regional Park.

The second weekend of August brings out flying daredevils at the Abbotsford International Airshow. In this aerial show, stunt flyers perform a reenactment of Pearl Harbor, complete with explosions for dramatic effect. Aerobatic teams, state-of-the-art aircraft and the Canadian Snowbirds demonstration team also take part in the annual event.

The vivid green Thompson River merges with the dark Fraser River in the semi-arid Fraser Canyon. Meeting at Lytton, 175 kilometres northeast of Vancouver, the two rivers contribute to one of the largest watersheds in Canada. Simon Fraser named the Thompson for explorer David Thompson. Later, Thompson returned the favour and named the province's longest river in Fraser's honour.

Rafters on the 489-kilometre-long Thompson River challenge the currents.
Some of Canada's best whitewater rafting rivers are within a few hours'
drive of Vancouver, among them the Fraser, Thompson and Chilliwack.

Index

Acknowledgements

Long Beach Helicopters is pleased to sponsor this book since it shows the views that we, as pilots, experience daily and at times may take for granted.

Long Beach Helicopters started operating in 1976 from a base at the Tofino Airport on the west coast of British Columbia. In 1980, the company opened a second base in Nanaimo and most recently a third one in Campbell River. We operate Eurocopter AS 350Bs exclusively because they are reliable, comfortable and safe.

Our helicopters have operated in almost every province in Canada and we have been involved in fire fighting, surveys, forestry, mining, communications, tourism, medical evacuations, aerial photography, motion picture photography, and more. In the last few years, we have provided specialty tours such as heli-fishing, wildlife viewing, flights over the Inside Passage and wilderness areas not accessible by other means.

Long Beach Helicopters would like to thank various government agencies, mainly NAV Canada for its support in directing traffic and providing aircraft separations on photo shoots around Victoria and Vancouver.

Long Beach Helicopters can be reached at 2363 Cienar Drive, Nanaimo, BC V9T 3L6. Telephone: (250) 758-0024. Fax: (250) 758-2531.